Stock Market Investing For Rookies

Go from Rookie to Rock Star with this Complete Stock Market Investing Guide for Absolute Beginners.

Jake Doxon

Copyright© Jake Doxon

All Rights Reserved

INTRODUCTION
- THE BIG MONEY MACHINE

CHAPTER ONE
- WHAT PRECISELY IS A STOCK?

CHAPTER TWO
- YOUR FIRST STOCKS
  - *So how precisely do I purchase a stock?*
  - *Do I use a GTC order or Day order?*

CHAPTER THREE
- PROFIT FROM ETF'S

CHAPTER FOUR
- PROFIT FROM DIVIDEND STOCKS

CHAPTER FIVE
- PICK STOCKS LIKE WARREN BUFFETT

CHAPTER SIX
- VALUE INVESTING AND P/E'S

CHAPTER SEVEN
- PROFIT FROM GROWTH STOCKS

CHAPTER EIGHT
- PROFIT FROM IPOS

CHAPTER NINE
- PROFIT FROM A STOCK THAT IS GOING NOWHERE

CHAPTER TEN
- THE SMART DAY TRADING STRATEGY

CHAPTER ELEVEN
- FIVE HUGE MISTAKES THAT BEGINNERS MAKE
  1. Don't purchase stocks that are hitting 52-week lows

2. *Don't trade penny stocks.*
3. *Don't short stock*
4. *Don't trade on margin.*
5. *Don't trade others' ideas.*

CHAPTER TWELVE

INSIDER SECRETS OF THE STOCK MARKET
About the author

INTRODUCTION

THE BIG MONEY MACHINE

The stock market is perhaps the best money machine created by man for man. I created this book so that everybody can approach the stock market, not just the rich and advantaged.

There is a spot for everybody in the stock market. You can put resources into stocks, hold them for a long time and stash the profits in your bank account afterwards.

You can likewise trade stocks. You can swing trade, day trade, or short them (bet that a stock will go down rather than up).

Let no one define your limits when it comes to the stock market. Subsequent to digesting this book, you may even think of your own unique method of benefitting from the stock market that nobody has at any point thought of previously.

In this book, I will give you a range of strategies you can deploy to profit from the stock market. At the point when you are first beginning, you should practise various methodologies and see what works for you.

We all have different mental make-up and appetite to risk. Some people want to be in the thick of things in the area of day trading. Others simply are cool with getting rich gradually and discreetly with no pressure. There is space for the two kinds of individuals in the stock market.

I would simply ask you to figure out how the stock market really function. Many individuals never set aside the effort to become familiar with this. Countless individuals like to tell the stock market how to work.

The stock market is a complex developing framework. It will not pay attention to you or to any other person. It simply does what it does, so you should become familiarised to it. Set aside the effort to figure out how the stock market truly works.

This is significant on the grounds that we live in a world driven by financial markets. On the off chance that you can learn even a small part of how it works, you can give yourself a tremendous leverage throughout life.

To rehash what I said toward the start of this book:

The stock market is one of the best opportunity ever known to man.

Tragically, the vast majority never figure out how to saddle this opportunity to make riches.

You are not the vast majority.

You bought this book because you were attracted to the promise in the book.

If you have big plans for your life in terms of making a lot of money, and you are willing to learn how to trade and invest, then I am willing to take you by the hand and show you the ropes. I want to be instrumental in helping you get rich.

The stock market has been immensely great to me. I'm at where my greatest objective is to help many people achieve impressive success in the stock market. That is the reason throughout the previous few years, I have been showing others how to trade and invest through my books.

So read this book gradually, and soak up the secrets. Go over it again and then again read it at whatever point you need a little motivation. I composed it for the individual who knows close to nothing or nothing about the stock market, however has enough curiosity to learn.

CHAPTER ONE

WHAT PRECISELY IS A STOCK?

A stock is a share or portion of ownership in a company. At the point when I purchase 100 shares or portions of Amazon, I become a part owner of the company and described as a "shareholder."

If I had sufficient money, I could essentially purchase up every share of Amazon, and afterward I would become the sole owner of the company. I would be the head of the eCom giant.

Here's another perspective to consider this picture. Amazon resembles a pie that has 500,000,000 slices (shares). As I am typing these words, every one of these slices is priced by the market at $3656.64 that is what we mean when we say that the stock is trading at $3656.64.

Now, we should take the absolute number of slices and multiply by the cost per share. We get about $1.83 trillion. That is the current absolute value of this "pie" that we call Amazon. Another term for this is "market cap" or "market capitalization."

At the point when we heard that Apple had become the greatest company in history, we normally imply that it has the highest market cap among other companies.

On 2 August 2018, Apple made history. It became the first trillion dollar company and made history again on 4 August 2020 to hit 2 trillion dollars.

Today, 29 July 2021, its market cap is $2.48 trillion making it the world's most valuable company by market cap.

A company's market cap and stock price will move around much over the long haul. Establishing a company's worth takes a lot of processing of data by people and machines. By purchasing or selling a company's stock, these brokers and investors push a stock's price to what it currently commands due to known data about the company.

Once in a while the market is wrong on the value of a stock and company. In 1999, etoys.com was estimated to worth $165 million when it went public in May of that year with a share selling for $76.50 on the day of IPO. In Feb 26, 2001 the shares of the company was halted by the stock exchange when it was selling for 9 cents per share as the company announced that it shares has no value.

In 1996, Apple was worth under $3 billion. Then, at that point the company brought back Steve Jobs, who presented the iPod and the iPhone.

The cost of Apple's stock (and henceforth its market cap) first leisurely (and afterward immediately) increase as the market sorted out how effective and beneficial these gadgets would be.

The stock market changes with new data. That is one thing that makes stocks move around. Stocks additionally move dependent on the laws of demand and supply.

When many people wants to purchase a stock, the price will climb. Perhaps those individuals are excessively idealistic, yet their purchasing will still make the stock move up. Then, at that point if a big investor comes in and begins to dump his stock, the price of the stock will drop down.

In some cases it is a mystery why a stock is trading up or down. In the long run it eventually becomes clear.

The stock market attempts to sort out what is destined to occur in the next 3-6 months, and afterward set stock prices in line with that. That is the reason we say that the stock market is a "forward-looking system" or "discounting system."

In 2009, the U.S. economy was not doing well. People were losing their homes and jobs. All things considered, the stock market started to record a climb. Then, at a point it started picking up steam. This confused many people who could clearly see all the signs of a bad economy. But the stock market was right as it signalled a recovery in the economy.

A similar sort of thing can occur with an individual stock not just the entire economy. Now and again a stock will report extraordinary income (for example tell everybody that it had a decent quarter and raked in some serious cash), yet at the same time, the next day. The share price will take a fall. It does this since traders are responding to something different in the profit call or in the company forward-looking remarks. The stock is "skating" to where the company will be in a couple of months.

A novice trader will be enticed to purchase a stock like this when it is down, yet this is quite often a poorly conceived move. It can require some time for new data to get valued into a stock, which implies that this stock could keep on moving lower for quite a long time, maybe weeks or months.

The opposite can likewise occur. A company may report a lot higher than anticipated income. The following day, the stock gaps up (opens up a lot higher than where it was trading the earlier day). Then, at that point the stock keeps on moving higher for a couple of days, or even weeks.

This happens in light of the fact that the large institutional players (hedge funds, pensions and mutual funds) are purchasing more portions of the stock and driving it nearer to its new "reasonable worth" dependent on the new data that turned out in the profit report and call. At the point when one is purchasing millions (or even billions) of dollars' worth of stock, as these players usually do, one can't do it like a push of a button. It can require hours, days, or even weeks.

In a later section, I will demonstrate how you can profit by exploiting these sluggish, ambling goliaths. However, I'd prefer you learn the fundamentals at the moment.

In the following section, I will tell you the best way to open up a brokerage account and purchase your first stock.

CHAPTER TWO

YOUR FIRST STOCKS

Some individuals like to purchase stocks and hold them for a long time. We call them "Investors."

Others like to purchase and sell stocks on a short time basis, perhaps holding them for just 60 minutes, a day, seven days, or a month. We call these individuals "traders."

Both are entirely acceptable approaches to profit in the stock market. A few investors make jest of brokers, and the other way around. I would ask you not to pick any side.

I'm both an investor and trader. I like to have different game plan running at the same time – short term, long term as well as a mix of options, bonds, venture capital, currencies, futures and real estate.

You should attempt the various game plans that I depicted in this book, to find what works out best for you based on your risk tolerance and individual psychology.

Make sure to talk with a qualified financial advisor before attempting any investment journey.

Then, at that point when you are prepared, you will face the question:

So how precisely do I purchase a stock?

Stocks are typically purchased and sold on what are known as "stock exchanges." A stock exchange is just a place where sellers and buyers come to exchange 'money for shares' or 'shares for money.'

The most notable exchanges in the U.S. are:

- The New York Stock Exchange (NYSE) and
- The NASDAQ.

The NYSE is most popular for its blue chip stocks like Coca-Cola and McDonald's. The Nasdaq is famous for hosting tech stocks like Apple and Netflix.

NYSE stocks are generally recognized by a two-letter "ticker" or (stock symbol) like HD (Home Depot) or KO (Coca-Cola).

Nasdaq stocks normally have four-letter tickers like AAPL (Apple) or NFLX (Netflix). A few times you'll likewise track down a two-letter ticker on the NASDAQ like FB (Facebook).

Stock exchange, those days is where you also find a ton of men standing on a floor with little stack of paper and shouting buy and sell orders. Presently everything is run by a computer. The computers coordinate sellers and buyers who need to trade their stock for money (or the other way around) at a specific price.

As an individual, you can't just buy a stock on a stock exchange like buying groceries in a store. For that you will require a "broker" or "brokerage account."

A broker is essentially a middle man between individuals and the stock exchange. In the U.S., notable brokers are Interactive Brokers, TD Ameritrade, Charles Schwab, TradeStation, Fidelity, and E*Trade.

My number one agent is Robinhood.com . They make it truly simple for amateurs. You go to their site, fill out a little online form, at that point move some cash into your recently opened brokerage account. Robinhood.com is extraordinary on the grounds that they permit you to purchase and sell stocks without paying a commission (expense).

Whenever you open up your brokerage account, it's an ideal opportunity to purchase your first stock. Here are two easy to follow videos to guide you

https://youtu.be/if1lxuHa-ZM

https://youtu.be/pDuIvrirPPc

At the point when you are purchasing a stock, you will be given the decision of utilizing two types of orders. The first is known as a "market order." This request advises the broker to get you into the stock as fast as could be expected, paying little mind to cost. On the off chance that you go with a market order, you may wind up purchasing the stock at a price that is far away from where it last exchanged.

This is on the grounds that each stock has a bid price and an offer (or "ask") price. The bid is the price at which somebody will purchase the stock. The 'ask' is the price at which somebody is willing to sell the stock. Remember this:

'You buy from the ask and sell to the bid'

The distance between the bid and the 'ask' is known as the "bid-ask spread." A liquid stock like Apple (AAPL) will have a bid-ask spread from simply a penny. So this moment as I'm composing these words, there is somebody at the bid for Apple who will purchase 2,000 shares for 144.98. Also, there is somebody at the 'ask' who will sell 1,000 shares for 144.99. That is a bid-ask spread from simply a penny ($0.01).

A liquid stock is characterized as a stock where you can purchase or sell a ton of shares without moving the stock price excessively. Liquid stocks in the U.S. normally have a bid-ask spread from simply a penny or two.

In the event that you submit a market order to purchase a liquid stock, you will for the most part be OK. That is on the grounds that a market order will advise the broker that you need to purchase your shares from the ask. Since it is only a penny away from the bid value, your request will generally be filled extremely near what the stock price is currently commanding.

Notwithstanding, on the off chance that you utilize a market order to purchase an illiquid stock, you may get it at a price that is far away from the current market, or from what the stock last exchanged.

Suppose that stock XYZ is illiquid. There's a bid for only 600 shares at 25.00. Furthermore, there's an ask for 400 shares at 26.00. On the off chance that you utilize a market order on a stock like this, you will have your request filled at 26.00 or higher.

Let's assume that you put in a market order for 800 shares on XYZ, your broker will initially give you the 200 shares at 26.00. Then, at that point they will search at the following best prices. In an illiquid stock, that may be one more 200 shares at 26.125 and afterward one more 200 offers at 26.25. So you will wind up getting 800 shares of XYZ at a average cost of 26.09375.

Presently suppose that you no longer want the shares and need to quickly sell your stock. In the event that you submit a market order to sell, you can initially offer 600 shares to the bid at 25.00. Then, at that point there is a bid of 200 shares at 24.75. In case you are filled at these prices, you will wind up having lost $925 (before commission), despite the fact that the stock has not actually moved.

That is the reason it is normally best to avoid illiquid stocks. On the off chance that you cannot avoid trading them, you can have a limit order put directly in the middle of the bid-ask spread. However, there is no assurance that your request will at any point be filled.

2. A limit order is the other kind of order, next to a market order. Though a market order advises your merchant to simply get you into or out of the stock as quick as could be expected without minding the price as much, a limit order is very specific about price.

So let's assume you submit a limit order to purchase AAPL stock at 144.98, your request might be filled in case there is a dealer that is willing to give up their shares at that price. In case there is no dealer willing to sell at that price, your order won be filled.

Limit orders are great for trading fluid stocks. So assuming I need to purchase a fluid stock like AAPL, I will look where the 'ask' is, and afterward enter a limit order utilizing that ask price. That way I will not stumble into difficulty if a whiff of market-moving news comes out one millisecond after I submit my request and AAPL abruptly spikes to 150.98 In the present circumstance, on the off chance that you have utilized a market order, there is a decent possibility that you will get filled at 150.98, despite the fact that Apple is a fluid stock.

At the point when you submit an order to purchase or sell a stock, you will have one more decision to make:

Do I use a GTC order or Day order?

A Day order may be executed during standard market hours today. On the off chance that the order has not been filled when the stock market closes for the day, it will be consequently cancelled by the broker.

A GTC ("good until cancelled") order will be useful for the present market hours, even till the next coming days and weeks. On the off chance that you didn't cancel it, it will still be working. A few brokers will consequently cancel a GTC order following a month or so if it has not been filled, depending on their policy. Check with your specific broker to learn more about their policies.

Standard trading hours for U.S. stock trades like the NYSE and Nasdaq are 9:30 am EST to 4 pm EST. A few brokers will allow you to exchange stocks during the pre-market exchanging hours (4 am to 9:30 am EST) or in the post-market exchanging hours (otherwise called "after-hours trading" and spanning from 4 pm to 8 pm EST).

In case you want to trade before the market opens or in the after-hour market, consistently utilize a limit order.

Indeed, even a typical liquid stock can be very illiquid (and thus unpredictable) during both of these exchanging sessions. "Unpredictable" implies that the stock squirms around or hops around a great deal. You may see a XYZ stock exchanging for 105, then, at that point 107, then, at that point 102, then, at that point back to 105.

Stocks with lower trading volume will ordinarily be more unstable, with a wide bid-ask spread that likewise bobs around.

Until you become a highly skilled trader, it is most likely best to adhere to typical market hours. What's more, never trade an IPO utilizing market orders. That is a serious amateur flop. More on that in a later section.

CHAPTER THREE

PROFIT FROM ETF'S

Now that you've opened up a brokerage account, you are prepared to purchase your first stock. Which stock would make a good pick for you to purchase?

Various investors decide to purchase an index, as opposed to a getting just one stock. an index is essentially an assortment (or "basket") of stocks. Suppose that we take the 500 U.S. stocks with the biggest market caps and throw them into a big bucket. That bucket is known as the S&P 500.

(Note: index like the S&P 500 are market-cap weighted, which implies that the companies in them that have bigger market caps are given higher weightings and in this way impact the index greatly. On the off chance that Apple has an awful day, the S&P 500 will go down more than if a Company like Gap Inc. or Under Armor has an awful day You can see the relative weightings here:

https://www.slickcharts.com/sp500

You've likely known about 2 other index (plural is "indices").

There's the Dow Jones Industrial Average (DJIA). This is a well-known index that started back in 1896. It generally contains just 30 companies. Now and again a company gets kicked out, and another one added.

August 24, 2020, Honeywell, Amgen & Salesforce joined the Dow, as replacement for Raytheon Technologies, Pfizer and Exxon-Mobil.

At the point when you hear on the news that the "Dow" was down 300 points, this is the index that is being alluded to.

The 30 Dow stocks are generally extremely huge and notable companies. At times individuals call them "blue chips" or "blue chip stocks" since they are mature, huge, profitable, and genuinely stable companies. To see which stocks are at present in the Dow, you can go here: https://en.wikipedia.org/wiki/Dow_Jones_Industrial_Average#Components

Another notable index is the Nasdaq 100, which contains on the most part tech companies. You can see its present members here:

https://en.wikipedia.org/wiki/NASDAQ-100#Component

Most Nasdaq 100 companies can be thought of "blue-chip companies" also.

Assuming you needed to purchase stocks into an index like the S&P 500, you would have to purchase every one of the 500 stocks simultaneously. That would be a tall one to execute. Luckily, there is a simpler method to do it.

Some savvy guys created the ETF ("exchanged traded fund"). ETF trades actually like a stock. You can buy or sell it any time of the day in your brokerage account. Every ETF addresses a specific list. So the ETF designated for the S&P 500 trades under the ticker SPY. The ETF assigned for the DJIA trades under the ticker DIA. What's more, the ETF for the Nasdaq 100 trades under the ticker QQQ.

You've presumably known about the QQQ, if not no problem. It is an incredible investment or trading vehicle. At the point when you purchase shares of the QQQ, you are getting access to Apple, Netflix, Google, Amazon, Facebook, and numerous other tech (and some non-tech) stocks. In the event that you purchase the QQQ and hold it as long as possible, you will actually benefit from the profitability of the tech industry.

You've likely likewise known about indexing. It comprises of purchasing an index (normally like a ETF like the SPY or QQQ), and holding it as long as possible. Indexing is a type of "passive investment." Passive investing alludes to any system that doesn't include a ton of thinking, buying and selling and all that activity in between (for example you don't bother much with the question "which stocks should I purchase today?")

At the point when you index, you simply purchase whatever stocks are in the index. You simply sell a stock when it gets kicked out of the index. Furthermore, you could purchase a stock when it gets added to the index. Or then again you simply purchase the SPY or QQQ, and these index changes are worked in automatically for you.

Today indexing is broadly viewed as the most secure and most ideal way for the vast majority to put resources into the stock market. In the event that you own the S&P 500 list, you are fundamentally assured to get a similar long haul return of the U.S. huge cap stock market.

Long before now, not many individuals did any indexing. That assured that it would give very great returns. Nowadays, somewhere in the range of 50-70% of the cash in the stock market is attached to indexing. This more likely than not guarantees that speculation returns won't be as great in the future as they have been before.

That being said, the vast majority lose cash when they attempt to trade or invest all by themselves, so its best they have some type of indexing methodology.

Truth be told, active investing methods are difficult to master as opposed to passive investing methods like indexing.

A great many people don't do what it takes to learn the ropes to acquire the active investing skills.

When indexing, a great many people like to contribute an equal dollar amount of cash into an index each month. That way, you never purchase the entirety of your stock at the top of the market. By purchasing a stock or index/ETF at various occasions, you are making price average out. By doing this, you wind up getting a very decent "average price." That is the reason this strategy is classified "cost averaging."

Another approach to index is to purchase a low cost or minimal expense mutual fund like the Vanguard 500, which just charges you a cost proportion (yearly expense) equivalent to 0.04% of your investment. By contrast, the SPY ETF charges an expense ratio of 0.0945%, however it permits you to trade in and out of the stock during the day.

Unlike like the Vanguard 500 that just permit you to purchase or sell shares once a day dependent on closing market price.

Most investors can start out with the SPY, since you can invest as little as two or three hundred dollars. Right now, to put money into the Vanguard 500 mutual fund, you should have a minimum $3,000. Purchasing a stock index like the S&P 500 is an extraordinary method to begin investing. In the event that you can, you should simply get some SPY and not bother with it for the next 30 years. At the point when you are indexing, you don't want to be checking the stock activity daily.

That being said, an extraordinary chance to put resources into an index like the S&P 500 is during a bear market. In the event that stock costs have been falling for half a year or more, and there is a ton of signs that things will not pick up soon, that may well your opportunity to put some additional cash into index. This is on the grounds that lower stock price will permit you to purchase more shares of stock for a similar dollar sum than you could if stock costs were higher.

Let's talk about dividend investing.

CHAPTER FOUR

PROFIT FROM DIVIDEND STOCKS

Dividend stock will generally make a money instalment into your brokerage account at regular intervals say quarterly. That cash instalment is known as a dividend.

Putting resources into dividend stocks is one smart road to riches. The good thing is that you can take the money from a dividend payment and plough it back to purchase more dividend stocks. Then, at that point those dividend stocks will deliver you more dividends.

In the event that you continue to do this over many years, you will wind up like Ronald Read. He spent half of his life as a gas station attendant and the other half as a Janitor yet this guy amassed wealth at the later end of his life. He led an uncomplicated, frugal life and channelled a lot of his earnings into dividend stocks. At the point when he passed on at 92 years old, he left behind a $8 million fortune, all in dividend stocks.

Ronald Read legacy remind us that you don't need to come into a lot of money before you can become a millionaire. You simply need to spend less than what you earn and put the rest in dividend stocks.

At the point when you own dividend stocks, the money hits your brokerage account like clockwork, whether you have a job or not. It's somewhat similar to renting out a property, the checks just keeps coming. The best thing about dividend stocks is that the management and staff of the company do the work, while you just wait for your checks.

Suppose that you purchase a dividend stock XYZ at $50 per share that pays you

$0.5 like clockwork (quarterly):

$0.5 paid multiple times each year is $2.0. That is your yearly all out in profits.

Presently take $2.0 isolated by the value that you paid for the stock ($50):

$2.0/$50 is 0.04 or 4%.

4% is the thing that we call the stock's "dividend yield." If you put your cash in a savings account, you may make 2% yearly. That is your savings account's yield.

Communicating things as far as yield permits us to think about various investment and compare them. For this situation, the dividend stock has a better return than the bank account, which is something worth being thankful for. Notwithstanding, when you purchase a stock, it can generally go down in price and make you lose cash. That doesn't happen with a savings account.

A profitable company will raise its dividend each year. Suppose that the non-existent company referenced above raises its dividend each year by until it started offering twice as much than the first year you bought the stock. Following 10 years of doing this, the yearly profit instalment will move from $2.0 to $4.0. You paid only $50 for each share, so presently your profit yield is 8% (4.0/50). The more you hold a dividend stock like this, the higher your yield becomes.

Warren Buffett purchased Coke in 1988. His compelling dividend yield today on those shares is more than 60%. As such, he presently gets more in Coke profits each 1.7 years than the dollar amount he paid for those stocks. That is one explanation why that man is a billionaire.

Coke is an exceptional sort of dividend stock. It is a Dividend Aristocrat, one of a first class companies that have raised their dividends each year for as far back as 25 years. Other Dividend Aristocrats on the list are Colgate-Palmolive Company, Johnson and Johnson, and McDonald's.

There's a simple way to possess a piece of each Dividend Aristocrat: simply get a few shares of NOBL. It represents the ProShares S&P 500 Dividend Aristocrats ETF. It trades actually like a stock, and you can buy it utilizing any brokerage account.

Thinking about what amount a company (like Apple) delivers in dividend?

Simply head over to Google and type in: "What amount does Apple deliver in dividend?"

To deliver a dividend, a company should be profitable. Once in a while a company will take a loan to pay its dividend, however that can never keep going for very long.

Dividend are normally paid out of a company's steady cash flow. One of the extraordinary things about putting resources into dividend stocks is that you realize that the company is banking huge bucks else it wouldn't have the option to pay you at regular intervals.

Possessing a string of dividend stocks over a significant stretch of time is extraordinary compared to other approaches to create wealth.

And if you start on time, you may even wind up with millions like Ronald Read.

CHAPTER FIVE

PICK STOCKS LIKE WARREN BUFFETT

Whenever I hear Warren Buffett talk about his investment strategy, he generally made it to appear to be so simple. You simply purchase stocks from a good company at a reasonable price and hold for the next 50 years.

It seems like anybody might have seen that Coca-Cola would have made a fabulous selection. However, how many individuals you know of that have held Coca-Cola shares since 1988 (which is when Buffett got it)?

In the realm of investment, we are compelled to consider what's to come. Investing like Buffett is not a walk in the park. You need to pick companies that will do well (and continue to do so for a long time. What's more, you should be mindful so as not to overpay for these stocks.

Those are not easy to implement strategies even Warren Buffett periodically gets it wrong at times, as he as of late confessed to overpaying for Kraft-Heinz.

That being said, there's a truly simple approach to pick stocks like Warren Buffett: Just copy the man.

Check out the web link to read up the recent letter sent out

http://www.berkshirehathaway.com/letters/letters.html

Look down and you will see a rundown of each stock that Buffett claims. For the 2020 letter, you can peruse this rundown on page 6 of the PDF. It incorporates the accompanying stocks and more:

AbbVie (ABBV)

American Express (AXP)

Apple (AAPL)

Bank of America (BAC)

Charter Communications (CHTR)

The Coca-Cola Company (KO)

Moody's (MCO)

Chevron Corporation (CVX)

Merck & Co. (MRK)

Probably the coolest thing about this rundown is that you can utilize it to compute the actual value that Buffett paid for each stock. Simply take the "cost" for each stock and divide it by the "number of shares."

Buffett has held the majority of these stocks for a long time, so you most likely will not get an opportunity to buy any of them at his costs. That being said, every so often one of his new picks will fall beneath his price tag, and you will have the chance to buy a few shares at a lower cost than Buffett himself paid. Smart people do that over time and you are welcome to join the league.

You could likewise purchase a bucket of these stocks that Buffett claims. Purchase the bucket of stocks, and afterward sell a stock just when you hear that Buffett has left the position.

A significantly simpler course may be to simply get some B-shares of Berkshire Hathaway (ticker: BRK-B). One share of stock in this company will cost you $279.40 today. You would then be able to take it easy and let Warren Buffett, Charlie Munger, and, their management do the difficult work for you.

On the off chance that you study Warren Buffett for a long time as I have, you will start to see that his stock picks follow a specific format.

They are typically solid, famous brands like Coca-Cola and Apple. He likewise prefers to get stakes in financial corporations like Bank of America, American Express, and the likes- - presumably on the grounds that these companies rake in some serious cash during the good times. They likewise get bail out by the government authority during the bad times.

Recollect that Buffett is the quintessential insider. He's not simply a folksy clodhopper who lounges around eating burgers and drinking coke the entire day. He gets access to legitimate privilege information not available to you or me.

That being said, there's one significant exercise that we would all be able to gain from Buffett's investment style. You need to possess shares in companies that have great pricing power. This implies that they can raise prices without losing customers.

At the point when Coke chooses to raise its price by a dime for every can, you likely don't take note. Be that as it may, when your neighborhood corner store is priced dime over its rival, you will presumably go to the rival all things being equal.

It's very hard to get rich in a price competitive business. In the event that you sell corn, oil, or conventional apparel, you have a great deal of cut-throat competition, and your margins are razor thin.

Then again, let's assume you have a big brand or can make a one of a kind item, you have less competition and you can command higher margins. Assuming somebody needs an Apple PC or a couple of Nike shoes, there's just one spot to get them. That is the reason Apple and Nike can charge premium for their goods.

As Buffett says:

The absolute most significant item in assessing a business is pricing power. In the event that you have the ability to raise prices without losing business to a contender, you have an excellent business. The opposite holds true.

CHAPTER SIX

VALUE INVESTING AND P/E'S

At its most fundamental level, value investing is simply purchasing something for short of what it is worth. It is an extremely profitable technique, since who doesn't prefer to get an incredible bargain?

Several years ago, the well-known financial investor Benjamin Graham and Warren Buffett raked in tons of cash utilizing an exceptionally variant of this strategy.

They would search a company that had net value of $20.00 per stock, and afterward attempt to purchase shares of that stock for $15. All in all, they were attempting to purchase a dollar for 75 pennies, or even less. Or on the other hand they would simply purchase stock in a company that had a P/E of only 5 or 6.

P/E is a term that means "price to earnings ratio." Let's say that a company stock trades for $100 and that the company has earnings per share (EPS) of $6.50 in the past twelve months. We can ascertain the following, P/E, for that stock by just computing the stock price ("P") by the EPS ("E"), so we get 100/6.50 giving us a value around 15.

We can say that this stock has a TTM P/E (trailing twelve month price to earnings ratio) of 15, that figure is a very decent average P/E for a stock or for even the stock market overall.

Companies that are growing their incomes or making profits rapidly ("growth stocks") will in general have P/E's over 25. Thus, for instance, today Microsoft has a P/E of 38.98 and Amazon has a P/E of 68.5

Companies that are in a difficult situation regularly have P/E's under 10. And some of such companies never get to recover again.

Today individuals regularly mistake value investing for purchasing stocks with low P/E's. As I referenced earlier, that worked admirably in the past when Warren Buffett was a youngster, however it quit working years ago.

Until you become a highly skilled investor, never purchase a stock with a P/E of 10 or less. It's simply a terrible spot to fish in. It is loaded with companies with bloated debts, dwindling revenues, or obsolete products that innovation have moved past. Also, likely a couple of fraudulent companies too. So stay away.

Another slip-up that new investors make is purchasing "bargain stocks."

Low P/E stocks are quite often courting bad news. You should never hope to discover great stocks in the bargain dumpster —except if maybe you are toward the finish of a multi-year bear market. And, after all said and done, you are better off purchasing a promising company that has a higher P/E.

Allow me to give you a case study. In late 2009, you could purchase shares of Blockbuster at a P/E of 2. Or on the other hand you could purchase shares of Netflix at a P/E of 26.

Ponder which one ended up being the better speculation?

Blockbuster was exchanging at a P/E of 2 since its profit were going to totally vanish soon. Netflix was trading at multiple times its present earnings. And as time went on, its income is about to shoot up than what was the case.

Netflix proceeded to take pretty much each and every Blockbuster customer.

In 2009, Netflix had profit of $116 million. In 2018, Netflix had income of $1.2 billion. On 28 December 2009, Netflix had a market cap of generally $3 billion. That implies that on the off chance that you purchased a share of Netflix stock toward the finish of 2009, you were in a real sense getting it at a future P/E of 2.50 (that comes down to $3 billion divided by $1.2 billion).

As we referenced previously, in case you will be a decent investor, you need to figure out how to think like Wayne Gretzky: you should "skate" to where earnings will be, not to where they have been.

Incase profit will fall, that P/E of 8 that you are paying may end up being a P/E of 100. On the off chance that the company is sinking toward insolvency, common shareholders investors will lose out and the debt holders will possess and control the company. That implies that your stock will become zero.

Bringing out cash for a stock that will eventually worth zero is never a decent move. We call these circumstances "traps." They look like great deals, however they end up being traps.

A former hot tech company is never a decent deal when its share price has fall from grace. Think Yahoo or Blackberry.

A low or falling stock price will make it hard for the company to draw in top talent. A company's stocks don't only mirror its present possibilities, yet it additionally predicts its future possibilities. A company with a high or rising stock price can utilize that stock to push out competition and pay for top talent. That is how Facebook managed Whatsapp and Instagram.

At the point when you are simply beginning, it is best to trade growth stocks and momentum stocks. It is possible to make good cash with value investing, however you need inside out information on the company's health status and have a pulse on the future condition of its industry.

Innovation and technology as well as changing customer tastes (think, Millenials and Generation Z) are making it progressively tricky to foresee what's to come.

I trust that subsequent to the information you found in this book. You won't ever purchase a stock just because it is "cheap" or has a low P/E.

CHAPTER SEVEN

PROFIT FROM GROWTH STOCKS

Growth stock is basically the stock of any company that is likely to quickly grow and increase income or revenue.

Here's the main principle to keep in mind when trading growth stocks:

Overlook the high P/E.

Promising companies that are growing quickly will consistently come with high P/E's.

They probably won't have any income. They may be losing a great deal of cash as they grow their share in the overall industry, a good example was Uber. They may even grow their share of the overall industry for a long time, before they turn on the profit faucet. That is the thing that Facebook did. It grew the social network for a long time, before at last turning on advertising.

Value investors will consistently advise you to avoid companies with high P/E's or companies that are losing cash. However, in the event that you do that, you will pass up the absolute most prominent stock runs ever. Microsoft, Starbucks, Home Depot, and Amazon all traded at extremely high P/E's for a long time. Amazon actually does till date. In any case, these stocks have proceeded to make their holders exceptionally rich.

Companies with high P/E's are tying their high growth to future income. In the event that it seems as though growth is easing back or that those income may never show up, the market will dump the stock. That is the reason we generally trade growth stocks with an unmistakable stop loss.

In case you are Warren Buffett putting resources into a mature companies, in that case the P/E matters. In case you are holding a growth stock for half a month or even months, nothing could matter less than the P/E.

Allow me to clarify how to trade growth stocks in my perspective:

It's good to purchase from the stocks that are hitting new 52-week highs, or even all new high.

This may appear to be nonsensical to a few. Isn't it unsafe to purchase a stock that is at record-breaking new highs? Doesn't that imply that it has a long way to fall?

In the event that you study the best growth stocks of the past, you will start to see that they spend a good chunk of time trading at record new highs. This bodes well basically on the grounds that any stock that goes up a great deal should (nearly by definition) invest a good chunk of time trading at new highs.

For what reason would you at any point need to pass up one of such opportunity, just on the prejudice against high P/E's or a dread of purchasing a stock at a record new high?

There is, truth be told, something great and amazing about a stock at a record-breaking high:

Each and every holder of the stock has a profit.

On the other hand, when a stock has slumped or is continually hitting new 52-week lows, there are numerous investors and dealers still have the stocks. On the off chance that the stock, attempts to get back up, these investors will be glad to get out by selling their shares at their break-even price. This gives consistent descending pressure, and accordingly makes it harder for the stock to get back up.

At that record breaking price, everyone that holds such a stock has a profit. There are almost no losers or those who are afraid to hold onto the stock: they have all left at one point or the other before the new high. At new highs, there are just cheerful and enthusiastic investors left.

Indeed, with the exception of one group of investors that nobody feels a lot of compassion toward - the short-sellers. These are investors who have shorted the stock (most likely in light of the fact that "it has a high P/E") and are betting that it will go down. At another unsurpassed high, every individual who has shorted the stock beforehand now has a losing trade on their hands. They are breaking out in cold sweat.

What's more, there's only one thing that they can do to stem their losses or make some profit: they attempt to "cover" their shortage by repurchasing the stock. This purchasing just adds more fuel to the fire, driving the stock higher, and pushing out more short-sellers.

In the interim, a stock that has as of late climbed a ton starts to be included on CNBC and examined by online pundits. This exposure acquires another flood of new purchasers, who keep on driving the stock higher and make it hit much more new unsurpassed highs.

I like to call these "growth stocks." One approach is by checking them continually when you scour the rundown of stocks at 52-week highs or new record-breaking highs, which you can check here:

https://www.barchart.com/stocks/highs-lows/highs?timeFrame=1y

The second stage is to consider the daily chart of each stock. You want to be sure that the stock is trading beyond its 50-day moving average; and that the 50-day moving average is beyond the 200-day moving average.

The upper line is the 50-day moving average, and the lower line is the 200-day moving normal. At the point when a stock resembles this, you realize that it is marking an uptrend.

Never purchase a growth stock if the stock is trading beneath its 200-day moving average, or on the other hand if the 50-day moving average is trading underneath the 200-day moving average. In the event that both of those two rules are valid, the stock is in a downtrend.

There isn't anything more troubling than a growth stock in a downtrend. A growth stock may go up 300% more than 3 years, and afterward fall 80-95% once it enters a downtrend. This can happen even with prominent companies. It happened to Cisco, Amazon, Crocs, and many different names.

In the event that a growth stock is trading beyond its 50-day moving average, and the 50-day moving average is trading beyond the 200-day moving average, it is a good sign.

In the event that the stock is trading at new 52-week highs or all-time highs, that is far better.

On the off chance that a stock shoots up to new highs after a solid earnings report, that can be a strong purchase signal. Because of an irregularity called "Post-Earnings-Announcement Drift" (PEAD), a stock that has gapped up like this will tend to keep moving up higher for a long time or even weeks. As an individual investor, you can ride the wave, as bigger institutional investors add to their portfolios over the long haul causing the stock to rise higher.

Sometimes, you may need to delay until the stock has been trading beyond the 50-day moving average.

In a solid market, you can likewise purchase each pullback to the 50-day moving average. This sort of trade has an incredible risk/reward ratio, since you can stop yourself if the stock really closes underneath the 50-day moving average.

There are a couple of more ways that we can apply with growth stocks.

Growth stocks perform much better when the whole stock market is in an upswing. In the event that the SPY and QQQ are trading over their 50-day moving average, what's more, if their 50-day moving average are over their 200-day moving average, it is a decent sign that the overall stock market is experiencing an uptrend. That upswing will add more fuel to push growth stocks higher.

Additionally, I like to search for growth stocks that have a market cap of $5 billion or less. It takes significantly less cash to push a $5 billion stock higher than it does a $500 billion market cap stock.

Numerous large hedge funds and mutual funds can't even consider a stock if its market cap is under $5 billion. On the off chance that you can enter the uptrend early, when the stock has a market cap of under $5 billion, you will be in a good place if the stock trades higher. When the stock ranges $5-10 billion market cap, there is a totally different set of institutional players who will start to consider that stock. As they buy shares, it will drive the growth stock much higher.

I additionally prefer to search for growth stocks, where the float is under 20% of the number of shares outstanding. The "float" is shares the quantity of a stock that are really accessible to the public for buying and selling.

To figure the float, you simply take the number of outstanding shares and take away the ones closely held by company insiders (those held by founders, employees, and unique investors that are secured and not open to be purchased).

You can go through this web link to look the float for any stock:

https://finance.yahoo.com/quote/UBER/key-statistics

This web link is set to Uber, yet you can go through it to look up any stock's float, just by changing the ticker in the URL. The float and total outstanding shares are recorded in the middle of the extreme right section.

Just click on statistics if your page open as summary

We can see from this web link that UBER right now has 1.88 Billion outstanding shares, however with a float of 1.64 Billion shares.

In any case, there are numerous growth stocks with little float that will go up a ton in case there is even a tad of interest. For instance, Twitter opened up to the world about a float of 11.38%.

Institutional and retail interest for the stock combined with the little float was sufficient to drive the stock price from 45 to 74 in a matter of weeks.

I additionally prefer to search for growth stocks with a high short interest. "Short interest" is the amount of shares that have been sold by the individuals who anticipate that the stock will go down. You can track down a stock's short interest here:

https://finance.yahoo.com/quote/UBER/key-statistics

Once more, you can change the ticker in the URL to look at some other stock. Look down the extreme right segment, and you will see "Short % of Float." This is basically the quantity of shares that have been sold short divided by the float (which we looked at previously). Some loathed stocks will have a short percentage as a level of float that is somewhere in the range of 10%-50%

Presently short sellers (traders who are wagering that a stock will go down) are generally smart. At the point when a stock continues to hit new 52-week lows and it has a high short interest, you need to avoid such stock.

Short sellers are not, be that as it may, reliable. Also, when a stock with high short interest begins hitting new highs, short sellers will be compelled to repurchase back their stocks, against their earlier speculation. At the point when they do, the stock price will move higher. High short interest is essentially more fuel for a growth stock's climb. That is the reason if a growth stock is hitting new 52-week or unsurpassed highs and it additionally has a "Short % of Float" that is around 10%, I get intrigued to buy. As the shorts gets pressed, a stock like this can at times climb 30% or more in an extremely brief timeframe.

We've invested some time examining when to purchase a growth stock. That is usually the most straightforward part of the story. Realizing when to sell (at either a profit or loss) can be trickier. Here is a list of the measures that I like to apply:

Take profit when you are so energized and glad about your trade that you are losing sleep for it.

Take profit if a stock goes up 100% in about fourteen days or less. Take profit when you are up 300% from your purchase price.

Take profit when everyone, CNBC and even your friends start to discuss a lot about the stock. Now, the trade has gotten swarmed, and things might get bad.

Take profit if a cab driver or hairdresser advise you to purchase the stock.

Exit (with a loss or profit) when the stock closes beneath its 50-day moving average. Utilize this technique to catch shorter moves.

Exit (with a loss or profit) when the stock closes underneath its 200-day moving average. Utilize this technique to catch longer moves.

Exit (with a loss or profit) when the 50-day moving average crosses beneath the 200-day moving average. Utilize this strategy to catch longer moves.

Utilize a 10-day or 20-day exponential moving average (EMA) as a tailing stop. Exit your position if the stock has a daily close underneath this EMA.

You can likewise scale out of a profitable position. Sell 25% of your position each Monday for about a month straight, or something almost identical. That is a decent method to secure a few profits, while as yet holding some of the stock in the event that it keeps on moving higher.

Simply make certain to never add to a losing position. Pick a stop loss level even before you enter the trade and stick to it. Growth stocks go up quick, yet they can likewise go down quick.

I generally prefer to commit only 1% of my trading account on each trade. Suppose that I am trading a $100,000 account. In that circumstance, I will bring out just 1% of my account, or $1,000. In the event that I enter the stock at 100 and the 50-day moving average is at 95, that implies that my risk is 5 points on the stock (100-95). All things considered, I should just purchase 200 shares of stock. In the event that I purchase 200 shares of stock, and the stock falls 5 points, I will have lost $1,000 or only 1% of my absolute account size.

The way to make money is to first not lose the money. At the point when you are first starting out as a trader, be certain not to make this flop. Keep your losses to a minimum and reasonable, particularly while you are as yet in the learning stage. It's OK to purchase only 1 share of stock when you are trying out a new strategy (particularly in case you are utilizing Robinhood and in this manner not paying any commissions).

CHAPTER EIGHT

PROFIT FROM IPOS

I'm regularly asked by new traders whether they should play IPOs. On the off chance that you know what you are doing, IPOs can be an extraordinary opportunity to rake in boatloads of cash. However, in the event that you don't, you will typically get your fingers burnt.

Allow me to clarify:

An IPO ("initial public offering") happens when a once privately owned business chooses to take on investors from the public. It does this by either having insiders (founders, directors, institutional investors and even venture capitalist) sell some of their shares to people in general, or the company gets to create new shares that's offered to the public.

Those shares are then, at that point "listed" on a public stock exchange like the Nasdaq or the NYSE where anybody can purchase or sell them. Initial public offerings gives the insiders a chance to cash out, while additionally fund-raising for the company to grow its operations.

There is typically a ton of publicity and media inclusion encompassing huge IPOs (think Facebook, Alibaba,

Budweiser, and Uber). This publicity assists with finding buyers for the recently issued stock.

Shockingly what regularly occurs in IPO is that insiders offer their shares to clueless retail investors. It very well may be a big move of wealth from "dumb money" (you and me) to the "smart money" (insiders, Big institutional players and VCs, etc) You will regularly get a whirlwind of IPOs toward the finish of a long buyer market, as we saw in 1999-2000, and same thing in 2019.

So in the event that you at any point purchase shares of an IPO, take a mental note of who you are purchasing from. You are purchasing from smart insiders who have a deep understanding of how the company works, its weaknesses and strengths, and its prospects.

The brilliant insiders may be selling their shares since they imagine that the company future prospects are poor. Or then again they may very well sell so they can purchase their own personal luxury plane and pent house.

In any case, IPOs can be an incredible trading vehicle for the highly skilled trader. This is on the grounds that IPOs as a rule have small floats and solid institutional backing, basically for the initial first six months.

As we referenced earlier on growth stocks, a little float implies that not the entirety of a company's shares are accessible to the public.

A little amount of IPO's shares are permitted to trade on the stock exchange, while the remainder of the shares are "secured" and can't be sold until the first six months elapsed.

Since there are not many shares accessible, it's a lot easier to move the stock up or down a great deal. That is the reason (LYFT) slammed so rapidly after its IPO. The company gave just 32.5 million shares out of a sum of 273 million outstanding shares.

That is an exceptionally small float - only 12% of its outstanding shares were accessible to be traded. A couple of days after its IPO, short-sellers jumped on LYFT, driving it down from a high of 88.60 down to the high 40's. It is currently at 56.

The opposite can occur with a little float. PagerDuty (PD) IPO'd in April 2019 by offering just 9.07 million shares to the general public, out of a sum of 73.6 million outstanding shares. That is a float of 12%. The stock began trading the high 30's, and immediately moved over to 50.

Additionally GoPro (GPRO) ran from 30 to almost 100 soon after its IPO, prior to slamming down. It presently trades around 10.

Twitter (TWTR) ran from 45 to 73 soon after its IPO, prior to smashing down underneath its IPO cost but its back up to 69.

There are 2 different ways to go about an IPO.

The principal way is as a long-term investor. In the event that you purchased 1 share of Coca-Cola for $40 when it IPO'd in 1919 and clutched it, your position would presently be worth more than $15 million (on the grounds that you utilized all dividends that the stock paid you to purchase more shares).

I wish that my granddad had done that, yet he didn't. On the off chance that you purchased shares of Walmart, Home Depot, Walt Disney, Starbucks, or Microsoft when they IPO'd and hung tight, you (or your grandkids) are rich in today standards.

Obviously, in the event that you purchased shares of Webvan (an online grocery company) at its IPO in 1999, your shares are presently worth zero. Webvan filed for bankruptcy in 2001.

It's difficult to overpay at an IPO, if the company will be around for the next 30 years and keep expanding its position. However, most companies don't become the next Microsoft or Starbucks, so you can't just purchase each IPO that comes out. There are too many IPOs, and a considerable lot of them will be bankrupt only 5 years after the fact.

To be a long term investor in an IPO, you need to know something about the business and furthermore have a right perspective on the company's future possibilities.

You then, at that point need to put the stock where you will not be enticed to trade it.

Indeed, even Coca-Cola's stock fell by 50% in its initial a year as a public company. Would you have the confidence to hang tight, watching your $10,000 venture become $5,000? That is simply the question you must have answered before you purchase an IPO fully intent on holding it for the next 20 years.

There's a further complexity today, companies used to launch an IPO a whole lot sooner in their business lifecycle.

Amazon was established in 1994, and IPO'd in 1997 (only 3 years after the fact). On the other hand, Uber was established in 2009, and didn't IPO'd until 2019 (after 10 years). Amazon IPO'd with a market cap of just $438 million. Uber IPO'd with a market cap north of $80 billion.

As companies stay private longer prior to having an IPO, the bulk of the profit will go to the private shareholders. Perhaps Uber will go from $80 billion to $800 billion (making 10x on your cash), yet it is unlikely, On the other hand, public investors had the option to benefit from Amazon's ascent from $438 million to over $900 billion (making 2052x on your initial investment). On the off chance that you purchased Uber at the IPO as a long term investor, you are likely the dumb money.

The second method to go about a IPOs is like trader. An IPO with a little float can possibly go up or down a lot, which makes it an extraordinary trading vehicle.

I would say, the more hyped an IPO is, the more effort it might take to make money from it on the long side. Be that as it may, I'm glad to short an over-hyped IPO, if the price action turns negative.

At the point when I'm purchasing IPOs, I like to zero in on more veiled companies, which I frequently find on this schedule of new IPOs:

https://www.nasdaq.com/markets/initial public offerings/

At the point when I am interested in a new IPO, I normally watch it for a few weeks, to have a feel of how it is trading. In the event that I feel that the S&P 500 is going to go down, I will frequently short a new IPO that has a small float (provided that I am able to borrow the shares to short). On the off chance that the S&P 500 goes down 10%, a new IPO may go down 50-75%.

Moreover, if the S&P 500 has been going down for a couple of months and my feelers reveal to me that it is near the bottom, I will proceed to purchase a new IPO with a small float. In the event that the S&P 500 spikes up by 10%, a new IPO could go up over 100%.

I additionally prefer to search for ongoing IPOs that are trading at a tight price range, with contracting volume. At the point when the IPO breaks out of this range with an accompanying expanded volume, I will go on to purchase the breakout and hold for a few weeks, utilizing a trailing stop.

For these sort of trades, as a rule utilize a 15-day exponential moving average (EMA) line as trailing stop. In the event that the stock closes underneath that line, I will promptly leave the trade.

Trading IPOs with a stop loss and solid discipline. Many individuals who purchased an IPO for a trade, overlooked their stop loss, and chose to clutch the IPO as a long term hold. Large numbers of those stocks end up going to nothing.

There is normally a "lockup" for IPOs. This implies that insiders can't sell any of their secured shares for the initial 180 days of trading (this is the reason new IPOs regularly have a small float). From that point onward, they are regularly allowed to dump the vast majority of their shares on the open market, which can at times make the stock go down pointedly.

In case you are trading an IPO, ensure that you know about when the lockup terminates. In some cases the termination of a lockup won't move the stock fundamentally. In some cases it will. That is the reason focus on the price action of a stock around its lockup.

CHAPTER NINE

PROFIT FROM A STOCK THAT IS GOING NOWHERE

Did you realize that there is an approach to benefit from a stock that is neither going up nor going down?

We should take stock XYZ which has been exchanging somewhere in the range of 45 and 50 for the last year. Suppose that the stock is as of now at 47.50. Presently suppose that we don't anticipate that the stock should move up higher or crash. We expect that the stock will keep on roaming along somewhere in the range of 45 and 50 for the next few months.

So we pay for 100 shares of the stock at 47.50, and promptly sell them in four months' time at 48.00.

We sell the call options for 1.25 per share, that means 100 shares of the stock costs us $4,750 (no commissions are charged in the event that we use Robinhood.com). By selling in four months' time at 48.00 call option, we are giving somebody the contract to purchase our 100 shares of XYZ stock from us at 48.00 whenever before or at the point the contract expires. Call options contract can last weekly, monthly or quarterly. In return for the contract, we will stash $125. At 1.25 per share, 100 shares of stock will bring in $125. We will keep this $125 regardless of what happens to the stock. We are likewise qualified for any dividends that the stock pays while we're holding it.

In the event that the stock go past 48 (the strike price of our call option) close to termination, the stock will get a new owner at 48.00 and $4,800 will be paid to us (100 shares times 48.00). We paid just $4,750 for the stock, so that gives us a profit of $50 on our stock ($4,800 less $4,750). Add that to the

$125 that we got from the call option, and you'll see we'll end up making $175.

You'll see that in this model, we sold something (a call option) that we didn't effectively own. Try not to stress over the technical jargons and all.

In the event that you want to do such a trade, simply make sure that you utilize a "sell to open" order when selling the call option. In the event that you choose to leave this position, you'll need to utilize a "buy to close" order to dispose of the call option. After this order is executed, you are allowed to sell your stock as you typically would. Just never sell your stock without first leaving the call position, or you'll land yourself in hot water.

At this point you've most likely understood that this kind of trade is known as a "covered call." You short a call, yet you are "covered" against a major loss at the same time possessing the stock. For each call that you need to sell, you'll need to purchase 100 shares of the said stock to make this work.

When entering a covered call position, do well to purchase the stock first, then, at that point sell the calls at a strike price that is slightly above the price point you purchased the stock. You could go with the 3 to 4 months out when picking the expiration for your call option.

Covered calls are a lot simpler than they sound. This is another of those situations where you can learn more by really doing it, than you can by reading up about it. As we referenced previously, covered calls work best when a stock is caught in a trading range.

In the event that you feel that a stock is going to go up a ton, you would prefer not to sell calls against it, since that will kill off your potential gain. In the event that you feel that a stock is going to go down a ton, you don't want to own such stock by any means. You'll bring in some cash on the short call option, yet lose much more if the fundamental stock goes down a ton.

In this section, I have given you the abridged version of the topic 'covered calls.' Look out for my other books to get the full version.

CHAPTER TEN

THE SMART DAY TRADING STRATEGY

Day trading is to any trade activity that includes purchasing and selling a stock on the same day.

A true trader won't keep a position over night. Many individuals attempt day trading and get their fingers burnt. That is the reason I need to give you a basic method that has worked superbly well for me over a long time.

This method exploits a fundamental truth of market structure that I mentioned in Chapter 1:

It takes some time for huge players to enter and leave their positions in the stock market. In the event that a mutual fund or hedge fund is holding millions of shares of the stock XYZ, it can't just leave its position by punching a button. On the off chance that XYZ has recently announced some really bad news in their last earnings report, the hedge fund is in a predicament. It will require hours, days, or perhaps weeks for the mutual fund or hedge fund to leave its position, contingent upon how fluid the stock is.

What's more, the case also holds true for a stock that has recently announced very good news in its most recent earnings report. When a hedge fund wants to add to its position or open a new position in that stock, it might still require hours, days, or weeks.

Fortunately individual traders like you and I can exploit these sluggish, ambling goliaths.

When we see their tracks in a stock's price behavior, we can step ahead of them and rapidly execute our little order. Our little order won't push the stock price anywhere. However, these hedge funds or mutual funds' large orders will make the stock keep on moving.

By hopping before a huge institutional player, we can join the party as the hedge fund or mutual fund keeps on pushing the stock up when it is purchasing, or down when it is selling.

How about we start with a case study. On 26 February 2019, Sea Limited (ticker: SE) the gaming company, closed at 16.20. In the after-hours, the company announced a better than anticipated earnings. How would we realize that the profit were surprisingly good? Since the following morning the stock opened 15% higher at 18.64. The stock kept on moving higher for the remainder of the day, shutting down at 21.99. As such, subsequent to gapping up, the stock climbed another 18% during the day.

Here's a day trading tactic that attempts to catch moves like this:

1. Find a stock that is gapping up based on good news (like a surprisingly good earnings report).

2. Wait 15 minutes after the market is open, and note the stock's price around then.

3. Put in a limit order to purchase the stock at that cost.

4. If your request isn't executed in the following 15 minutes, cancel your order and leave.

5. If your order is filled, clutch the stock for the remainder of the trading day, and afterward take profits few minutes before the market shuts down for that day.

6. Exit the stock early on the off chance that it trades underneath the initial least price of 15 minutes of early daytime trading.

It's that straightforward. This tactic exploits a stock's inclination to continue to move in the direction of its morning gap, as big institutional players like hedge funds and mutual funds add to their positions.

What is a gap? It's basically when a stock goes up or down abruptly, leaving a "gap" or blank space on the charts that shows the distance between the past trade point.

CHAPTER ELEVEN

FIVE HUGE MISTAKES THAT BEGINNERS MAKE

In this chapter I will share many of the mistakes traders and investors make. You do well to avoid all these goofs, that way you will be way ahead of others and you will be on your way to making boatloads of cash instead of losing a lot of money.

Here are 5 rules you don't want to ever forget.

1. Don't purchase stocks that are hitting 52-week lows.

2. Don't trade penny stocks.

3. Don't short stocks.

4. Don't trade on margins.

5. Don't trade others' ideas.

1. Don't purchase stocks that are hitting 52-week lows

We have effectively talked about this point, yet it bears rehashing, basically on the grounds that a lot of new traders lose a ton of cash attempting to catch a "falling knife." regardless of what everybody will advise you, you are quite often much better purchasing a stock that is hitting 52-week highs than one hitting 52-week lows.

Has a company you own stocks in just revealed some bad news? You can be sure there are others you are not privilege to have. There's never just one cockroach in the kitchen if you start looking around. Bad news are like gangs. It's not just one, there is more. Investors in General Electric learned this the hard way when the company kept bringing bad news in bits by bits over a period making the stock decline from 30 to 7. There is nothing like a "safe stock." Even a blue chip stock can go down a great deal in the event that it makes a bad decision or loses its competitive advantage.

Of course bad news about a company can make a stock plummet down to a great extent. On the off chance that you own a stock that does this, it is smart to get out and stay out by a couple of months (or a long time) before you re-enter (buy that stock again). Again, there will never be only one cockroach.

Never purchase a stock after you have seen the first cockroach. At the point when a stock goes down a ton, it can influence the company's core. Board members and employees' confidence will take a blow, the best skilled talents may start leaving, and it might turn out to be harder for the company to fund-raise by selling shares or taking on debts.

On the other hand, when a stock goes up a ton, it can work in favor of the company's fundamentals. Board members and the employees are in high spirits, everybody at the company will need to work more diligently, it will be easier to enlist new talent, and it will become easier for the company to fund-raise by giving stock or taking on debts.

In the event that you have stocks that are trading higher than their 200-day moving average, or that are hitting 52-week highs, you will be smiling instead of attempting to catch falling knives.

2. Don't trade penny stocks.

A penny stock is any stock that trade under $5. Except if you are a highly skilled trader, you ought to stay away from all penny stocks. I would stretch out this by urging you to likewise keep away from all stocks selling under $10.

Regardless of whether you have a little trading account ($5,000) or less, you are in an ideal situation purchasing less shares of a more expensive stock than a ton of shares of a penny stock.

That is on the grounds that low-valued stocks are regularly connected with lower quality companies. Thus, they are not permitted to exchange on the NYSE or the Nasdaq. All things being equal, they exchange on the OTCBB ("over the counter notice board") or Pink Sheets, the two of which have considerably less rigidity in terms of regulation than the significant exchanges demand.

Large numbers of these companies have never made a profit. They might be outright frauds or shell companies that are planted exclusively to make company insiders and management become rich. Penny stocks could also involve stocks from former corporate giants (blue chips) that have lost their glory like Eastman Kodak or Lehman Brothers.

Furthermore, penny stocks are intrinsically more volatile than more expensive stocks.

Consider it along these lines: if a $100 stock moves $1, which is a 1% move. In the event that a $5 stock moves $1, that is a 20% move. As a new broker you are oblivious to the emotional upheaval and discomfort that sort of unpredictability can cause.

I would say, penny stocks don't trend anywhere close to more costly stocks. They will in general be more mean-returning (Mean inversion happens when a stock manoeuvres up pointedly from its average trading price, just to fall directly down again to its average trading price). Large numbers of penny stocks are heading eventually to zero. Most brokers won't allow you to short them. What's more, regardless of whether you do track down a broker who would let you short a penny stock, or the one time you find a broker who would let you short it only to find that the price has jumped by 400% which means you will pay four times the price of what you intend to short.

As if that is not enough trouble already, a penny stock may give off an impression of being fluid one day, and the following day, only for the liquidity to be short lived when you are up against a wide bid/ask spread. Or on the other hand the bid may totally vanish, that means there are no buyers for your stock. Imagine holding a stock that no one wants.

Avoid all stocks under $10. Likewise avoid trading newsletters that sell penny stocks. The proprietors of these bulletins are regularly paid by the actual companies to publicize their stocks. Or on the other hand they may take a position in a penny stock, fire an email advising everybody to get it, and afterward sell their stock at a lot more exorbitant cost to these novice purchasers.

3. Don't short stock

In case you are a high skilled trader, this point do not apply to you. In case you are not, I would truly urge you not to overlook this point.

To short a stock, you initially borrow a stock from your broker. You then, at that point can sell those shares on the open market. In the event that the stock falls in price, you can purchase those shares at a lower price and make some profit. Assuming that the stock goes up a great deal, you might be compelled to purchase the stock at a lot higher price cost, and wind up losing more cash than you anticipated.

A number of persons have got into trouble for this and end up losing their savings, homes and end up penniless and in debts.

In November 2015, Joe Campbell broke 2 of the 5 rules. He originally chose to trade a penny stock called KaloBios Pharmaceuticals. To compound the situation, he chose to short it.

At the point when he headed to sleep that evening, his trading account was worth generally $37,000.

At the point when he woke up the following morning, the stock had soar. Subsequently, not just had he lost the entirety of the $37,000, yet he presently owed his broker an extra $106,000.

Furthermore, there was no chance to get out. In the event that you owe your broker cash, they can pull you into court and take your home and savings.

Here and there even the most affluent investors can be become a pauper overnight out by shorting a stock. During the incomparable Northern Pacific Corner of 1901, portions of that railroad stock went from $170 to $1,000 in a one day. That move bankrupted probably the most affluent Americans of the day, who had shorted the stock and were then compelled to cover at the new high price.

In the event that you do wind up shorting a stock, recall that your broker will charge you an expense (normally withdrawn as a yearly fee) to get the stock. Furthermore, in case you short a stock, you are answerable for paying any dividends on that stock (your broker will naturally collect the cash from your trading account quarterly).

For these reasons, shorting stocks is unmistakably a high level and tricky thing. Try not to attempt it until you've been trading for somewhere around 5 years, and you have the financial backing to withstand an extraordinary upwards move in a stock.

What's more, never short a penny stock. It's a no go area. You should not even buy one.

4. Don't trade on margin.

To short a stock, you should open up an account with your broker. You'll likewise require a margin account to trade stocks using margin.

At the point when you purchase a stock on margin, it implies that you are borrowing cash from your broker, to buy a larger number of shares than you would ordinarily have the option to purchase with the money sitting in your trading account.

Suppose that I have $10,000 in my margin account. Most brokers in the U.S. will permit me to go on margin to buy $20,000 worth of stock in that account. This means they are loaning me an extra $10,000

They might charge hefty price of like 11%, for that service so I can purchase more shares of a stock.

In the event that I purchase $10,000 worth of stock and the stock goes up 10%, I've made a decent

$1,000. Yet, in the event that I can purchase more stock that I'm purchasing with $20,000 utilizing a margin advance, I will have made $2,000 on a similar 10% price upward move. That will imply that my trading account has neatly gone up by 20% ($2,000/$10,000).

Obviously, if the stock goes down 10% and I'm on full margin advance, I will have lost 20% of my total.

Trading on margin has both its advantage and the disadvantage.

At the point when you purchase a stock utilizing margin, the stock and money in your trading account is held as security for the margin credit. In the event that the stock falls enough, you might be forced to inject more money to your account quickly (this is term as "getting a margin call"), or risk having the broker force you to hawk your stock to raise cash quickly.

At the point when you want to open a brand new brokerage account, and you are given the option of a "cash account" or a "margin account," it's fine to pick "margin account." A margin account enjoys certain benefits, for example, having the option to utilize the returns from selling off a stock to quickly purchase another stock without waiting days before this can be done if it was a cash account.

In the event that you never spent past your money in a margin account, you won't ever be charged expenses or premium. In that manner, it's very conceivable to have a margin account, without the need to go on margin.

Assuming, in any case, you don't want to tempt yourself, open up a "cash account." That way, you won't ever be tempted to trade on margin.

To study how Robinhood handles margin, you can go here: https://support.robinhood.com/hc/en-us/articles/360026164112

5. Don't trade others' ideas.

There are two primary justification for this.

The principal reason never to trade another person's ideas is that they likely don't have a clue what they are talking about. In the event that you get a hot stock tip from your neighbor or at the barber shop, it's ideal to overlook it.

They presumably have no clue about the thing they are discussing.

Second, regardless of whether you get a great and real trading tip from another person, you will most likely not have the conviction to execute it when troubles arise. That conviction comes from developing your own thoughts and experience yourself. At the point when you have planned a trade, or investigated a stock for yourself, you will have the conviction to hang on. You will likewise know where your stop loss is, in the event that the stock goes south. Additionally, hot stock tip usually don't come with stop loss suggestion.

Likewise, never place a trade dependent on something that you have recently read in Forbes, Barron's, The Wall Street Journal, or have recently seen on CNBC. Never purchase a stock dependent on a some analyst update, or sell a stock dependent on an analyst downgrade.

I've seen analyst at long last downgrade a stock just when it has fallen 50%. The opposite also holds true. Analyst lag behind a great deal. They are outdated indicators.

Additionally, analyst fall for selection bias, and you can be negatively impacted listening to them. The best analyst get employed by mutual funds, and you never hear from them again. The most noticeably terrible analyst you can find at the banks or brokerage houses, and they keep on feeding their second rate advice to gullible persons. Fortunes have been lost following their recommendation.

Would it be advisable for you to try and follow Warren Buffett's recommendation? Yes, and no. His recommendation is certainly far superior to a hot stock tip from your neighbor or barber. Then again, on the off chance that you paid attention to him strictly, you would pass up the entirety of the incredible tech stocks of the recent two decades or more. He delayed in buying stocks in Apple and Amazon until they were commanding a high price before jumping in.

Anybody can figure out how to think for themselves in the stock market, and concoct their own trading and investing strategy. That is the objective behind the entirety of my books.

Maybe than giving you a fish, I would much prefer show you how to look for yourself. That is the way to genuine independence from the rat race.

CHAPTER TWELVE

INSIDER SECRETS OF THE STOCK MARKET

In this section, I will share some extremely important truths that you will read for the first time or that have been mentioned before but worth repeating.

Allow me to begin by helping you to remember the main facts about the stock market:

Response (reaction) that trail the news is in every case more significant than the actual news.

Thus, likewise:

Response to a positive earnings report is in every case more significant than the earnings report itself.

It's quite often a negative sign when a stock tanks after a decent profitable earnings report. In the event that a stock that has had a major run-up falls on a decent earnings report, it very well might be an indication that the uptrend has ended.

It works the same way the other way around. At the point when a stocks rises in price after a "bad" earnings report, it is a bullish sign. It's likewise a bullish sign if the stock market rallies after a negative economic report.

A lot of people expect the market to behave the way they expect. Shrewd traders pay attention to the market and not dictate for it.

Since you need to cash out today, it doesn't imply that the chance will be readily available. You should figure out how to be happy with what the market is presently offering you.

Try not to force a trade. Be patient, and sit tight for the fat pitch. If you can bring yourself to learn discipline and patience, the market will ultimately reward you beyond anything you could ever imagine.

Zero in on a couple of stocks, and become more acquainted with how they trade. Try not to extend yourself excessively far by attempting to follow a large number of stocks.

On the off chance that you have made a blunder, cut your losses fast and move on. Never let a trade turn into a long term hold/investment. Don't try to average losses. It's no use throwing good money after bad. Never add to a losing position, yet go ahead and add to a position once it begins to bring in cash.

The stock market is sometimes termed a discounting machine. That implies that it takes all accessible information about a company and the economy and fine tune a stock's price appropriately. At times it makes a better fine tuning than other occasions. The stock market tends to over-discount identified risks, and under-discount unidentified risks.

At whatever point you catch wind of a risk in the financial news, it is undoubtedly been factored into a stock, or the stock market overall. It is the risk that you are not hearing anything about, or that appear to be ridiculously improbable, that can cause the most harm. In case everybody is talking about something, chances are that it has been evaluated into the market. That implies that the stock has effectively moved to where it should be, founded on the entirety of the available information. As we referenced previously, to bank profits in trading or investing, you need to skate to where the puck will be, not to where it has already been.

A market that tries several times to move higher but fails each time will eventually go down. The stock market (just as individual stocks) will consistently look out for weaknesses, and move so as to distribute the most pain to the greatest number of traders.

Mass psychology might control the markets in the short term, but not the fundamentals or the economy. Upgrading the fundamentals of a company combined with great financial news in the economy will reflect in the stock price before they feature in the news, which is the reason you should carefully mind price action.

When the market is going up, and your stock is doing the same, don't be in a rush to take profit. To win at this match, you should have some big winners. Try not to interfere with them too early.

Seasons impact the stock market that we ought not disregard that fact. For example the two most well-known stock market crashes both happened in October (1929 and 1987), September has proved to be the weakest month from stock market history. Average documented returns for June and August are usually negative.

There's a famous saying to capture this sentiment "Sell in May and go away."

Stock market yield from November through April have verifiably been higher than yield from May through October.

This doesn't really imply that you should sell the entirety of your stocks and cash out each May. Yet, it implies that you ought to be more careful when trading throughout the late spring months. Many brokers and investors are chilling at the beach, hence lower liquidity and higher volatility.

In case you are searching for a decent stock to hold for the long term haul purchase a company that has the highest sales in its industry. So for home improvement, you need to go with Home Depot; for fast food, McDonald's; for toothpaste, Colgate Palmolive; for payments, Visa; for smartphone, Apple; and for social media, Facebook. When a business sells more than its competitors in its industry, it turns out to be a tall one for any competitor to beat. There's not a viable alternative for being #1 in your industry.

At the point when all the gurus agree, then, at that point something else will happen next. The current standard thinking that is pervasive has already been factored into the market.

About the author

Jake Doxon is a passionate investor, trader and author with over 20 years of experience. He lives in the United States. He loves to assist everyday individuals with cutting edge knowledge on how investment work so they can overcome their under-earning challenges and become wealthy.

Take a lock at my other titles on investment. Life has a lot more to offer if we are bold enough.

www.ingramcontent.com/pod-product-compliance
Lightning Source LLC
Chambersburg PA
CBHW020454220526
45464CB00002B/985